First World War
and Army of Occupation
War Diary
France, Belgium and Germany

28 DIVISION
Divisional Troops
38 Field Company Royal Engineers
1 April 1915 - 31 October 1915

WO95/2272/1

The Naval & Military Press Ltd
www.nmarchive.com
Published in association with The National Archives

Published by

The Naval & Military Press Ltd

Unit 10 Ridgewood Industrial Park,

Uckfield, East Sussex,

TN22 5QE England

Tel: +44 (0) 1825 749494

www.naval-military-press.com

www.nmarchive.com

This diary has been reprinted in facsimile from the original. Any imperfections are inevitably reproduced and the quality may fall short of modern type and cartographic standards.

© **Crown Copyright**
Images reproduced by permission of The National Archives, London, England, 2015.

Contents

Document type	Place/Title	Date From	Date To
Heading	WO95/2272/1		
Heading	28th Division Divl Engineers 38th Field Coy R.E. Apr-Oct 1915 From 6 Division		
Heading	28th Division 38th Field Coy. R.E. Vol IX To Twenty Eight Div Ap 8 1-30.4.15 Apr-Oct 15		
Heading	War Diary 38th (Field) Company Royal Engineers From 1st April 1915 To 30th April 1915		
Miscellaneous			
War Diary	Armentieres	01/04/1915	06/04/1915
War Diary	Bailleul	07/04/1915	07/04/1915
War Diary	Ypres	08/04/1915	30/04/1915
Heading	28th Division XXVIIIth (Transfered From) Division 38th Field Coy RE Vol X 1-31.5.15		
Heading	War Diary Of 38th (Field) Company RE From 1st May 1915 To 31st May 1915 1st Volume		
War Diary			
War Diary	Ypres	01/05/1915	29/05/1915
War Diary	Herzeele	30/05/1915	31/05/1915
Heading	28th Division 38th Field Coy RE Vol XI 1-30.6.15		
Heading	War Diary Of 38th (Field) Company Royal Engineers From 1st June 1915 To 30th June 1915		
War Diary	Herzeele	01/06/1915	14/06/1915
War Diary	Dickebusch	15/06/1915	30/06/1915
Heading	28th Division 38th Field Coy R.E. Vol XII 1-31.7.15		
Heading	War Diary Of 38th (Field) Company RE From 1st July 1915 To 31st July 1915 Volume 1		
War Diary	Dickebusche	01/07/1915	14/07/1915
War Diary	Kemmel	15/07/1915	16/07/1915
War Diary	Locre	17/07/1915	18/07/1915
War Diary	Dranoutre	19/07/1915	31/07/1915
Heading	28th Division 38th Field Coy. R.E Vol XIII August 15		
Heading	War Diary 38th (Field) Company RE From 1st August 1915 To 31st August 1915 Volume 1		
War Diary	Dranoutre	01/08/1915	31/08/1915
Heading	28th Division 38th Field Coy R E. Vol XIV Sep 1 15		
War Diary	Dranoutre	01/09/1915	21/09/1915
War Diary	Merris	22/09/1915	26/09/1915
War Diary	Bethune	27/09/1915	27/09/1915
War Diary	Sailly-Labourse	28/09/1915	30/09/1915
Heading	28th Division 38th F. Co. R E. Oct 15 Vol XV		
War Diary	Sailly-Labourse Vermelles	01/10/1915	01/10/1915
War Diary	Vermelles	02/10/1915	05/10/1915
War Diary	Vermelles L'Ecleme	06/10/1915	06/10/1915
War Diary	L'Ecleme	07/10/1915	16/10/1915
War Diary	L'Ecleme Bethune	17/10/1915	17/10/1915
War Diary	Bethune	18/10/1915	18/10/1915
War Diary	Bethune Essars	19/10/1915	19/10/1915
War Diary	Essars	20/10/1915	22/10/1915
War Diary	Essars Lillers En Route	23/10/1915	23/10/1915
War Diary	En Route Marseilles	24/10/1915	25/10/1915

War Diary   Marseilles   26/10/1915 31/10/1915

WO95/2272(1)

WO95/2272(1)

28TH DIVISION
DIVL ENGINEERS

38TH FIELD COY R.E.
APR - OCT 1915

From 6 Division

28th Division

6th Division

121/5256

38th Field Coy: R.E.

To Twenty-Eighth Div. Ap. 8.

Vol IX 1-30 ...

Apr - Oct '15

Confidential

War Diary
of
38th (Field) Company Royal Engineers

from 1st April 1915 to 30th April 1915

WAR DIARY
or
INTELLIGENCE SUMMARY.
(Erase heading not required.)

Army Form C. 2118.

Instructions regarding War Diaries and Intelligence Summaries are contained in F. S. Regs., Part II. and the Staff Manual respectively. Title pages will be prepared in manuscript.

Hour, Date, Place	Summary of Events and Information	Remarks and references to Appendices

WAR DIARY or INTELLIGENCE SUMMARY.

Army Form C. 2118.

Instructions regarding War Diaries and Intelligence Summaries are contained in F.S. Regs., Part II. and the Staff Manual respectively. Title pages will be prepared in manuscript.

(*Erase heading not required.*)

Hour, Date, Place	Summary of Events and Information	Remarks and references to Appendices
ARMENTIERES 1-4-15	Company employed in making footboards, dugouts & pumps & making holes in piers of PONT-DE-NIEPPE. Loopholing houses at HOUPLINES. At night one section supervising & revetting in trenches of 17th IB. Civilians cutting & carting brushwood & making hurdles & fascines.	JMMagor
ARMENTIERES 2-4-15	Company employed in making hurdles, dugouts footboards pumps. Making holes in piers of PONT DE NIEPPE. One pier completed. Supervising Infantry making approach road & erecting wire entanglement at HOUPLINES. At night one section supervising in 17th IB trenches. One part to repair water supply of QUEENS WESTMINSTERS. Civilians cutting & carting brushwood & making hurdles & fascines.	JMMagor
ARMENTIERES 3-4-15	Company employed in making hurdles, dugouts footboards & pumps. Making holes in second pier of PONT-DE-NIEPPE. Supervising Infantry making approach road at HOUPLINES. At night one section to 17th IB trenches supervising & revetting.	JMMagor
ARMENTIERES 4-4-15	Company paraded for Divine Service & did not work.	JMMagor

WAR DIARY
or
INTELLIGENCE SUMMARY.
(*Erase heading not required.*)

Army Form C. 2118.

Instructions regarding War Diaries and Intelligence Summaries are contained in F. S. Regs., Part II. and the Staff Manual respectively. Title pages will be prepared in manuscript.

Hour, Date, Place	Summary of Events and Information	Remarks and references to Appendices
ARMENTIERES 5-4-15	Company employed in making hurdles, footboards, dugouts & pumps. Making holes in second pier of PONT-DE-NIEPPE. At night one section to 17th I.B. trenches extending new trench. Civilians cutting & carting brushwood & making hurdles & fascines. 2nd Lt. J.J. Tickell wounded by gunshot.	F.M. Mapin
ARMENTIERES 6-4-15	Company employed in making hurdles, footboards, dugouts & chevaux-de-frises. Making holes in second pier of PONT-DE-NIEPPE & loopholing houses at HOUPLINES. At night one section to 17th I.B. trenches extending trench. Civilians cutting & carting brushwood & making hurdles & fascines.	F.M. Mapin
BAILLEUL 7-4-15	Received orders to join 28th Division at YPRES. Company marched to BAILLEUL & went into billets (9 miles) arriving at 10 pm.	F.M. Mapin
YPRES 8-4-15	Marched to YPRES & went into billets (15 miles) arriving at 2 pm. Visited trenches in company with Trench Engineer.	F.M. Mapin
YPRES 9-4-15	Company employed in cleaning billets after occupation by French. Trenches not taken over by British.	F.M. Mapin

WAR DIARY or INTELLIGENCE SUMMARY.

Army Form C. 2118.

(Erase heading not required.)

Instructions regarding War Diaries and Intelligence Summaries are contained in F. S. Regs., Part II. and the Staff Manual respectively. Title pages will be prepared in manuscript.

Hour, Date, Place	Summary of Events and Information	Remarks and references to Appendices
YPRES. 10-4-15	Company employed in billet. One section to workshops getting machinery in order & cleaning up etc.	H.M. Major
YPRES 11-4-15	Company employed in shops making footboards. At night one Officer & section to ZONNEBEKE for work in trenches of 85th Brigade.	H.M. Major
YPRES 12-4-15	Company by day in workshops at YPRES making loophole frames, footboards, hurdles etc. At night one party sinking mine in M17 trench in conjunction with mines made by trench. One party supervising infantry in revetting & closing gaps in line.	H.M. Major
YPRES 13-4-15	Company employed in workshops making hurdles, loopholes & mending forge. One section at VLAMERTINGHE erecting shelters for horses on change of billets. In trenches at night building up parapets & draining communication trenches in night, centre shaft battalions. Sinking shaft for mine, sunk 10 feet.	H.M. Major

WAR DIARY or INTELLIGENCE SUMMARY.

Army Form C. 2118.

Instructions regarding War Diaries and Intelligence Summaries are contained in F.S. Regs., Part II. and the Staff Manual respectively. Title pages will be prepared in manuscript.

(Erase heading not required.)

Hour, Date, Place	Summary of Events and Information	Remarks and references to Appendices
YPRES 14-4-15	One section to VLAMERTINGHE erecting shelters etc for horses, remainder of company making hurdles, footboards, loophole frames etc. In trenches One party in right section mining mine advanced to 15'. One party in right section revetting parapets & improving communications. Two parties repairing parapets in Centre & Left sections damaged by shell fire	[signature]
YPRES 15-4-15	One section to VLAMERTINGHE erecting shelters for horses & one section making garage for GOC Division. Remainder in workshops making footboards, hurdles & entanglements. At 5pm orders received to improve roadway N.E of YPRES to take all arms by 7pm. This was done. In trenches mine advanced to 18'. parties revetting & repairing parapets. Preparing holes for charges as defensive mines in advanced sap at BROODSEINDE	[signature]
YPRES 16-4-15	One party making garage & one party completing shelters at VLAMERTINGHE. One party making bridge over ditch on ZONNEBEKE road to take diversion. Remainder in workshops making footboards hurdles etc. In trenches report received at 7-30pm that considerable	

WAR DIARY or INTELLIGENCE SUMMARY.

Army Form C. 2118.

Instructions regarding War Diaries and Intelligence Summaries are contained in F.S. Regs., Part II. and the Staff Manual respectively. Title pages will be prepared in manuscript.

(Erase heading not required.)

Hour, Date, Place	Summary of Events and Information	Remarks and references to Appendices
16-4-15 (contd)	damage had been done to trench 22 by Minenwerfer. A party of 10 cyclists sent to reinforce section in trenches who were employed in repairing this damage & also damaged trenches in right & left section	H.M. Mager
YPRES 17-4-15	One party to VLAMERTINGHE making garage remainder in workshops making footboards hurdles, pickets loophole frames etc. In trenches One party in right subsection mining. Two trench mines cleared of water & debris Three parties repairing parapets etc	H.M. Mager
YPRES 18-4-15	One party to complete garage remainder in workshops making trench stores. Work stopped in afternoon as company was ordered to stand by for special work at night which however was not required In trenches 1 Officer & 20 men to BROODSEINDE to make emplacements for trench mortar One party continuing mines One party repairing parapets in centre section One party laying charges for defensive mines in advanced sap of centre section	H.M. Mager

WAR DIARY or INTELLIGENCE SUMMARY

Army Form C. 2118.

Hour, Date, Place	Summary of Events and Information	Remarks and references to Appendices
YPRES 19-4-15	Company employed in workshops making hurdles, footboards, parados boxes, pickets & loophole frames. Lieut Osborn killed in trenches. In trenches one party mining in right section. Two parties assisting in revetting parapets & taking out saps in right & left sections.	[signature]
YPRES 20-4-15	Company employed in workshops making trench stores. In trenches one party mining. Two parties repairing parapets in centre of left battalion.	[signature]
YPRES 21-4-15	Company employed in workshops making trench stores. In afternoon moved into bivouac NE of YPRES owing to shelling. In trenches one party mining. Remainder repairing trenches & building traverses. One gel. charge in advanced sap blown up at the request of OC of Infantry battalion. A small amount of damage done to enemy's trench.	[signature]

WAR DIARY or INTELLIGENCE SUMMARY.

Army Form C. 2118.

(*Erase heading not required.*)

Hour, Date, Place	Summary of Events and Information	Remarks and references to Appendices
YPRES 22-4-15	Company employed in making "dugouts" in bivouacs as no work was possible in YPRES owing to shelling. In trenches one party mining & remainder repairing parapets damaged by shell fire. One Sergt wounded in trenches. One Driver killed & 4 men wounded in bivouacs.	F.M. Major F.M. Major
YPRES 23-4-15	Company standing to awaiting orders. One Officer & 40 men of 171st Mining Company to ZONNEBEKE to carry on mining. One Corporal wounded & one man killed of this unit. In trenches improving parapets little work done owing to Infantry standing to most of the night.	F.M. Major
YPRES 24-4-15	One section together with sections of 2nd KARE & 1st Northumbrian RE placing farm in C.28.d in a state of defence. Party collecting material for repairs of bridges over the Canal. In trenches no work possible. One Sapper killed by shell fire in bivouac & one Sergt & 3 men wounded.	F.M. Major

WAR DIARY
or
INTELLIGENCE SUMMARY.

Army Form C. 2118.

Instructions regarding War Diaries and Intelligence Summaries are contained in F. S. Regs., Part II. and the Staff Manual respectively. Title pages will be prepared in manuscript.

(Erase heading not required.)

Hour, Date, Place	Summary of Events and Information	Remarks and references to Appendices
YPRES 25-4-15	Company standing to. No work possible in trenches owing to Infantry attack etc. Mining section returned to headquarters as no work was possible.	J.M.Mornay
YPRES 26-4-15	Company moved trenches owing to shell fire. In trenches repairing parapets & making parados	J.M.Mornay
YPRES 27-4-15	Company standing by. At night making dugouts for 11th Bde. In trenches relaying trench dis troyed by trench howitzer. Capt Pyne slightly wounded in head	J.M.Mornay
YPRES 28-4-15	Company making dugouts for Headquarters 11th Bat and section night. In trenches repairing trenches.	J.M.Mornay
YPRES 29-4-15	One section at night loopholing houses in trenches of 11th Bde & one section repairing parapets in trenches of 84th Bde	J.M.Mornay
YPRES 30-4-15	Company standing by. In trenches building & reinforcing fire trenches & making parados	J.M.Mornay

J.M.Mornay
of 38 (Welsh) Coy

28th Division

121/5505

XXVIIIth (transferred from ~~6th~~) Division.

38th Field Coy R.E.

1 — 31.5.15.

Confidential

War Diary
of
38th (Field) Company R.E.
from 1st May 1915 to 31st May, 1915

1st Volume

Instructions regarding War Diaries and Intelligence
Summaries are contained in F. S. Regs., Part II.
and the Staff Manual respectively. Title pages
will be prepared in manuscript.

WAR DIARY
or
INTELLIGENCE SUMMARY.
(Erase heading not required.)

Army Form C. 2118.

Hour, Date, Place	Summary of Events and Information	Remarks and References to Appendices

WAR DIARY or INTELLIGENCE SUMMARY.

Army Form C. 2118.

(Erase heading not required.)

Hour, Date, Place	Summary of Events and Information	Remarks and references to Appendices
YPRES 1-5-15	Owing to heavy shell fire it was necessary to move bivouacs & Company were employed in making fresh dugouts. In trenches repairing parapets & making communication trenches	J M Mayne
YPRES 2-5-15	Party returned from ZONNEBEKE owing to adjustment of line. Remainder of company at work on retired line in front of FREZENBURG under O. of 55 (med) Coy	J M Mayne
YPRES 3-5-15	One section making trench stores at VLAMERTINGHE. Remainder standing by	J M Mayne
YPRES 4-5-15	One section making trench stores at VLAMERTINGHE. One section at night making dugouts for Div – 13 at POTIJZE. Remainder of company at night working on line for defence of YPRES from square I, b 93 to cross roads I 2 d	J M Mayne

WAR DIARY
~~INTELLIGENCE SUMMARY.~~

(Erase heading not required.)

Army Form C. 2118.

Instructions regarding War Diaries and Intelligence Summaries are contained in F. S. Regs., Part II. and the Staff Manual respectively. Title pages will be prepared in manuscript.

Hour, Date, Place	Summary of Events and Information	Remarks and references to Appendices
YPRES 5-5-15	One section making trench stores at VLAMERTINGHE. Mounted section moved to N of ABEELE. One section at night to trenches of 84th IB repairing parapets & draining trenches. Arrangements made to continue line for defence of YPRES but orders received just prior to moving off that company would not be employed in this line.	J.M.Magnum
YPRES 6-5-15	One section at VLAMERTINGHE making trench stores. One section at POTIJZE making dug outs for men of company who will live there for work in trenches. One section to 84th IB trenches making barricade across WIELTJE — FORTUIN road.	J.M.Magnum
YPRES 7-5-15	One section at VLAMERTINGHE making trench stores. Two officers & one section to live at POTIJZE for work in trenches. Employed in completing barricade & assisting Infantry to dig trench to connect with 4th DIV.	J.M.Magnum

WAR DIARY
or
INTELLIGENCE SUMMARY.
(Erase heading not required.)

Army Form C. 2118.

Instructions regarding War Diaries and Intelligence Summaries are contained in F. S. Regs., Part II. and the Staff Manual respectively. Title pages will be prepared in manuscript.

Hour, Date, Place	Summary of Events and Information	Remarks and references to Appendices
YPRES 8-5-15	One section at VLAMERTINGHE making trench stores. One section with 84th I.B. improving trenches in G.H.Q. line. Two sections at night in conjunction with 1st Northumbrian Field Co. & 2nd Rangers Rgt. digging a retired line from SAINT JEAN to N & E of POTIJZE WOOD. 200 bns Infantry put in dug-outs on this line, 1 Offrs, 2 trench, light-spring ways, searchlight section of 2 N.C.Os, 10 sappers, 1 driver, 2 trench lines, light-spring ways, found.	
YPRES 10-5-15	One section at VLAMERTINGHE making trench stores for 84th I.B. One section constructing dug-out for Hd. Qrs. 84th I.B. in I.B. By night One + a half section digging & wiring 3 supporting points in rear of front line, between VERLORENHOEK and WIELTJE. Party superintending cavalry digging rear line running from point on SAINT JEAN – WIELTJE road, ½ m. W. of WIELTJE to a farm 200 yd E. of POTIJZE WOOD.	W.O.R. No. 6
YPRES 9&11-5-15	One section at VLAMERTINGHE making trench stores. Two sections at night wiring the retired line dug the previous night & clearing foreground. At 11 pm 700 Cavalry arrived & dug a trench from WIELTJE to POTIJZE. 2 Sappers wounded	

WAR DIARY or INTELLIGENCE SUMMARY.

(Erase heading not required.)

Army Form C. 2118.

Instructions regarding War Diaries and Intelligence Summaries are contained in F. S. Regs., Part II. and the Staff Manual respectively. Title pages will be prepared in manuscript.

Hour, Date, Place	Summary of Events and Information	Remarks and references to Appendices
YPRES 11-5-15.	One section completing dug-out for Hd. Qrs. 84th I.B. in I/b. One party at VLAMERTINGHE cutting pickets etc. for wiring. One officer obtaining details of bridges 7 & 8 in I/d. By night one section working in 9th Cav. Bde trenches, between main roads YPRES-WIELTJE & YPRES-VERLORENHOEK, & wiring them ¼ mile E of WIELTJE & ¾ mile E of POTIJZE. Very little work done as cavalry covering party did not arrive till after 12 a.m. Party completing supporting point & connecting up with existing communication trenches.	W.O.C. LOR E.
YPRES 12-5-15.	One section at VLAMERTINGE making trench slabs for left sector of line occupied by 1st Cav. Div. One party running up timber to be stacked at bridges 7 & 8. By night 1 Section working in left sector, rebuilding parapet, etc.	W.O.C. LOR E.
YPRES 13-5-15.	One section making trench slabs at VLAMERTINGHE. By night whole coy in trenches of left sector working in conjunction with No 2 SIEGE COY R.A.R.E. Blown in portion rebuilt, support & communication trenches dug & improved, supervision of 300 infantry digging party.	W.O.C. LOR E.
YPRES 14-5-15.	One section repairing main road from I7a via I/d to crossroads at I2d. Party in trenches of left sector making barricade & entanglement across POTIJZE-VERLORENHOE & road	W.O.C. LOR E.

WAR DIARY
~~INTELLIGENCE SUMMARY~~

(Erase heading not required.)

Army Form C. 2118.

Instructions regarding War Diaries and Intelligence Summaries are contained in F. S. Regs., Part II. and the Staff Manual respectively. Title pages will be prepared in manuscript.

Hour, Date, Place	Summary of Events and Information	Remarks and references to Appendices
YPRES 15-5-15.	One section making trench stores at VLAMERTINGHE. One party collecting timber at bridges 7 & 8. Small party fitting boxes for guncotton charges for demolition of bridges 7 & 8. Party building magazine for explosives. 1 Officer reconnoitring on retired line from I.16.b to I.22.b. By night 2 sections working on above line. One melting up 600 x wire, other supervising infantry digging party of 600. One sapper wounded.	W.E.E. L O R E.
YPRES 16-5-15	During the day the company was employed on fatigues in bivouac. Charges for demolition of Bridges Nos 7 & 8 made up complete. Three Officers reconnoitring CANAL line from point where it curved YPRES-MENIN Canal in I.19.d.7.3 to MENIN Gate.	W. E. E. L O R. E.
YPRES 17-5-15	By day one section making trench stores at R.E. Park VLAMERTINGHE. One section working on portion of CANAL line between LILLE & MENIN Gates, making M. G. emplacements along ramparts & improving communication trenches. Eleven other ranks joined as reinforcement.	W. E. E. L O R. E.
YPRES 18-5-15	By night one section continued work along ramparts. Two sections employed on rampart defences between LILLE & MENIN Gate. Nine M. G. emplacements completed, also communication trenches to them. Dug-outs for detachment of two finished, & for three others commenced.	W. E. E. L O R. E.

(9 29 6) W 3332—1107 100,000 10/13 H W V Forms/C. 2118/10.

WAR DIARY
or
INTELLIGENCE SUMMARY.

(Erase heading not required.)

Army Form C. 2118.

Instructions regarding War Diaries and Intelligence Summaries are contained in F. S. Regs., Part II. and the Staff Manual respectively. Title pages will be prepared in manuscript.

Hour, Date, Place	Summary of Events and Information	Remarks and references to Appendices
YPRES 19-5-15	Whole company employed on rampart defences. 4 additional M.G. emplacements completed, & communication trenches to them dug. Five more dug-outs for detachments constructed. One Officer distributed company of Belgians along portion of line between YPRES- MENIN Canal & LILLE Gate. One Officer conducting representatives of 85th I.B. over rampart defences.	W. O. C. 2o R. E.
YPRES 20-5-15	Work on rampart line continued by whole company. Sixteen M.G. emplacements now nearly complete & communications. Latter need deepening in places. Dug-outs for detachments for 9 M.G's. strengthened to allow more earth to be placed on top.	W. O. C. 2o R. E.
YPRES 21-5-15	Whole company employed on ramparts. Eighteen M.G. emplacements & communications finished. Dug-outs for nine detachments completed, & for remainder under way.	W. O. C. 2o R. E.
YPRES 22-5-15	Party repairing flooring of bridge No 10, & worked on approaches to bridge No 11. Four signboards for latter were made. Remainder employed on fatigues & constructing dug-outs.	W. O. C. 2o R. E.
YPRES 23-5-15	Two sections at R.E. Park VLAMERTINGHE making trench stores & anti-gas bombs. One Officer obtaining information from 4th Divl. R.E. as to method of working searchlight. Two horses wounded by shell in picket line in early morning & had to be destroyed.	W. O. C. 2o R. E.

WAR DIARY
or
~~INTELLIGENCE SUMMARY.~~
(Erase heading not required.)

Army Form C. 2118.

Instructions regarding War Diaries and Intelligence Summaries are contained in F. S. Regs., Part II. and the Staff Manual respectively. Title pages will be prepared in manuscript.

Hour, Date, Place	Summary of Events and Information	Remarks and references to Appendices
YPRES 24-5-15	One section making trench stores at R.E. Park VLAMERTINGHE. Company left dug-outs about noon owing to heavy shelling. One sapper wounded. Battery R.F.A. was also ordered to take up a position at site of coy. dug-outs. New dug-outs constructed during evening & night near Chateau opposite level crossing on main road one mile W. of YPRES. One Officer making detailed sketch of Section of CANAL line between No 1 Bridge on YPRES-YSER Canal & MENIN Gate. During early morning some of the company had to leave dug-outs & place on respirators owing to effects of gas attack on front line. By night one Officer & 3 N.C.O's reported to 80th I.B. for superintending infantry working party.	W.L.C. L.R.E.
YPRES 25-5-15	One section reported to 84th I.B. to dig dug-outs for Bde. H.Q. but work not required. Work continued on new company dug-outs. By night 3 sections working with 80th I.B. constructing retired line on S. side of MENIN road, ½ mile W. of HOOGE. One section making sandbag barricade on MENIN road. One section making supporting point at farm in I 17 d. 5. 9 One section wiring front line N. of MENIN road. Two N.C.O's & one sapper wounded. Two Officers siting new line S. of MENIN road & distributing Inf. digging party of 500.	W.L.C. L.R.E.

WAR DIARY or INTELLIGENCE SUMMARY.

Army Form C. 2118.

(Erase heading not required.)

Hour, Date, Place	Summary of Events and Information	Remarks and references to Appendices
YPRES 26-5-15	At night four sections erecting barbed wire in front of line held by 8th Inf Brigade from ROULERS RAILWAY to Wood S of HOOGE about 2000x. One Officer & four men with party of Infantry reconnoitring & marking communication trench from GHQ line to front line N of MENIN ROAD. One NCO & two Sappers wounded.	JMR Major
YPRES 27-5-15	At night four sections employed in strengthening above line of wire. Two Sappers supervising Infantry digging above communication trench. One NCO & one Sapper wounded.	JMR Major
YPRES 28-5-15	At night two sections reconnoitring & marking out communication trench from front line to GHQ line - N of RAILWAY.	JMR Major
YPRES 29-5-15	Two Officers & one section supervising Infantry digging above trench. One Officer & one section reconnoitring & supervising digging of support & communication trenches just S of RAILWAY	JMR Major

WAR DIARY
or
INTELLIGENCE SUMMARY.

(Erase heading not required.)

Army Form C. 2118.

Instructions regarding War Diaries and Intelligence Summaries are contained in F. S. Regs., Part II. and the Staff Manual respectively. Title pages will be prepared in manuscript.

Hour, Date, Place	Summary of Events and Information	Remarks and References to Appendices
~~YPRES~~ HERZEELE 30-5-15	Company marched at 7-30 am to bivouac S of HERZEELE to go in Army Reserve. Distance 19 miles. Mounted section joined remainder of Company	J M Brown Major
~~YPRES~~ HERZEELE 31-5-15	Company employed in overhauling company equipment etc	J M Brown Major
1-6-15		J M Brown Major O.C. 3rd Field Coy

28th Division

~~6th Division~~

38th Field Coy: RE.

Vol XI 1 — 30.6.15

121/5829.

<u>Confidential</u>

War Diary of
38th (Field) Company Royal Engineers

from

1st ~~May~~ June 1915 to 30th June 1915

WAR DIARY or INTELLIGENCE SUMMARY.

Army Form C. 2118.

(Erase heading not required.)

Instructions regarding War Diaries and Intelligence Summaries are contained in F. S. Regs., Part II. and the Staff Manual respectively. Title pages will be prepared in manuscript.

Hour, Date, Place	Summary of Events and Information	Remarks and References to Appendices
HERZEELE 1-6-15	In reserve overhauling equipment wagons etc	H.M.Morgan
HERZEELE 2-6-15	In reserve.	H.M.Morgan
HERZEELE 3-6-15	In reserve. Instruction in bombs given to Officers & NCOs 84th Infy Brigade	H.M.Morgan
HERZEELE 4-6-15	In reserve. Instruction in bombs continued to Officers & NCOs 84th Infy Brigade	H.M.Morgan
HERZEELE 5-6-15	Company inspected by GOC 28th Divn.	H.M.Morgan
HERZEELE 6-6-15	Company attended church parade	H.M.Morgan
HERZEELE 7-6-15	In reserve making notice boards for Divn. One Officer to NAMES TINGUE for work under CE 2nd Army. Instructed Officers & NCOs of 83rd Brigade in bomb throwing	H.M.Morgan
HERZEELE 8-6-15	Continued instruction in bomb throwing of Officers & NCOs of 83rd Brigade	H.M.Morgan
HERZEELE 9-6-15	Making Notice Boards for 28th Divn. &	H.M.Morgan

WAR DIARY or INTELLIGENCE SUMMARY.

(Erase heading not required.)

Army Form C. 2118.

Instructions regarding War Diaries and Intelligence Summaries are contained in F. S. Regs., Part II. and the Staff Manual respectively. Title pages will be prepared in manuscript.

Hour, Date, Place	Summary of Events and Information	Remarks and References to Appendices
HERZEELE 10-6-15	In reserve	FMMagan
HERZEELE 11-6-15	Dismantling hut for 28th Divt	FMMagan
HERZEELE 12-6-15	Instruction in throwing bombs for 85th Inf Brigade	FMMagan
HERZEELE 13-6-15	Company attended Church parade	FMMagan
HERZEELE 14-6-15	One Officer reported to CE 2nd Corps for duty, received orders for two sections to march to KEERSEBOOM & remainder of company to DICKEBUSCH on the following day	FMMagan
DICKEBUSCHE 15-6-15	Two sections to KEERSEBOOM for work under CE 2nd Corps. Remainder of company marched to DICKEBUSCH & went into huts (distance 16 miles)	FMMagan
DICKEBUSCHE 16-6-15	Making trench stores for 2nd JB & one section at night assisting Infantry to improve parapets	FMMagan

WAR DIARY
or
INTELLIGENCE SUMMARY.
(Erase heading not required.)

Army Form C. 2118.

Instructions regarding War Diaries and Intelligence Summaries are contained in F. S. Regs., Part II. and the Staff Manual respectively. Title pages will be prepared in manuscript.

Hour, Date, Place	Summary of Events and Information	Remarks and References to Appendices
DICKEBUSCH 17-6-15	Making trench stores by day. At night one section improving parapets in 84=J.B trenches.	4mm mag
DICKEBUSCH 18-6-15	Making trench stores. At night one section improving trenches in 84=J.B trenches.	4mm mag
DICKEBUSCH 19-6-15	Making trench stores. At night one section superintending infantry digging support & communication trenches. One man wounded. Listening gallery under P3 trench advanced 16'	4mm mag
DICKEBUSCH 20-6-15	Making trench stores. Two sections rejoined company from KEERSE ROOM. At night one section supervising digging & improving support & communication trenches. Listening gallery under P3 advanced 6' total 21 feet. Shaft sunk for listening gallery in P4 P4A to a depth of 9 feet	4mm mag

WAR DIARY or INTELLIGENCE SUMMARY

Army Form C. 2118.

Hour, Date, Place	Summary of Events and Information	Remarks and References to Appendices
DICKEBUSCH 21-6-15	Making trench stores & mining cases. At night one section improving M.S. making support & communication trenches to P₄ & sapping to open parapet of P₃. One section improving Infantry improving & making VORMEZEELE switch through BOIS CONFLUENT. Mining gallery of P₃ advanced to 26 feet. P₄ advanced 7 feet from small shaft.	YMM mayor YMM mayor
DICKEBUSCH 22-6-15	Making trench stores & mining cases. At night one section improving M.S. on VORMEZEELE switch & improving parapets & trenches. Mining P₃ advanced to 28'. P₄ advanced to 12'.	YMM mayor

Hour, Date, Place	Summary of Events and Information	Remarks and References to Appendices
DICKEBUSCH 23-6-15	Making trench stores & battle headquarters in gol 84" J.B. No M.S. working parties available at night owing to relief of Brigades. Mining P_3 trench advanced to 35 feet very wet.	
DICKEBUSCH 24-6-15	Making trench stores & completing accommodation for gol 84" I.B. At night one section supervising M.S. in communication trench in rear of M. Mining P_3 advanced to a total of 37'. 83rd Brigade Section of miners taking over charge of this section. Gallery in M. taken over by 84" I.B. 2nd Lt Wilson & Whitehead joined the unit	

WAR DIARY
or
INTELLIGENCE SUMMARY.

Army Form C. 2118.

Instructions regarding War Diaries and Intelligence Summaries are contained in F. S. Regs., Part II. and the Staff Manual respectively. Title pages will be prepared in manuscript.

(Erase heading not required.)

Hour, Date, Place	Summary of Events and Information	Remarks and references to Appendices
DICKEBUSCH 25-6-15	making trench stores & mining cases. At night one section assisting Infantry to fix loopholes & improve trenches. Owing to heavy rain no R.E. working parties available. Mining M, ventilation improved & tunnel advanced to a total of 45'. P₂ advanced to 37'.	Y.M.Munro
DICKEBUSCH 26-6-15	making trench stores, mining cases &c. At night one section in P trenches improving parapets. Also supervising Infantry in VORMEZEELE switch. One section supervising R.E. in communication trench in rear of M.	Y.M.Munro
DICKEBUSCH 27-6-15	making trench stores & mending road. At night one section supervising Infantry on VORMEZEELE switch in BOIS CONFLUENT & improving parapets. One section superintending Infantry on communication trench in rear of M.	Y.M.Munro

WAR DIARY
or
INTELLIGENCE SUMMARY.
(Erase heading not required.)

Army Form C. 2118.

Instructions regarding War Diaries and Intelligence Summaries are contained in F. S. Regs., Part II. and the Staff Manual respectively. Title pages will be prepared in manuscript.

Hour, Date, Place	Summary of Events and Information	Remarks and references to Appendices
DICKEBUSCH 28-6-15	By day making trench stores & mining cases & repairing roads. By night one section superintending Infantry constructing communication trench in M1 & M5. One section supervising Infantry in VORMEZEELE ditch & assisting to improve parapet & make machine gun emplacement. M1 trench advanced 5 feet total length 54'. N4 shaft sunk to a depth of 12'	H/M Meyer
DICKEBUSCH 29-6-15	Making trench stores & mining cases. Another bound for trenches. Very wet at night no work possible. M1 trench advanced to 59'. N4 shaft sunk to a depth of 13'.	H/M Meyer

WAR DIARY
or
INTELLIGENCE SUMMARY.

Army Form C. 2118.

Instructions regarding War Diaries and Intelligence Summaries are contained in F. S. Regs., Part II. and the Staff Manual respectively. Title pages will be prepared in manuscript.

(Erase heading not required.)

Hour, Date, Place	Summary of Events and Information	Remarks and references to Appendices
DICKEBUSCH 30-6-15	By day making trench stores. Night: Supervising Infantry on communication trenches in rear of M₁ & M₅ & demolishing houses in VIERSTRAAT. Supervising Infantry on VOORMEZEELE switch & digging a trench in P₁. Night: Debris in P₃ & P₄ removed which had been caused by wet. M₁ advanced to 69' & T head 4'. N₄ shaft sunk to 13'.	[signature]

1/7/15

[signatures]

28th
6th Division

181/6149

38th Field Coy R.E.

Vol XII . 1 – 31. 7. 15.

Confidential

War Diary
of
38th (Field) Company RE

from 1st July 1915 to 31st July 1915

Volume 1.

WAR DIARY
or
INTELLIGENCE SUMMARY.

(Erase heading not required.)

Army Form C. 2118.

Instructions regarding War Diaries and Intelligence Summaries are contained in F. S. Regs., Part II. and the Staff Manual respectively. Title pages will be prepared in manuscript.

Hour, Date, Place	Summary of Events and Information	Remarks and references to Appendices
DICKEBUSCHE 1-7-15	By Day. making trench stores & overhead cover & machine gun emplacements in the trenches. By night fixing loopholes in trenches & supervising infantry in VORMEZEELE & VIERSTRAAT LINES & communication trenches	A.M. Magor
DICKEBUSCHE 2-7-15	Day Trench stores & mining cases night supervising infantry as above	J.M.Magor
DICKEBUSCHE 3-7-15	as on 3-7-15	J.M.Magor
DICKEBUSCHE 4-7-15	Day Trench stores & mining cases & clearing in front of VIERSTRAAT LINE night. Supervising infantry on communication trenches & VIERSTRAAT & VORMEZEELE lines & erecting brushwood screens on communication trenches	J.M.Magor

WAR DIARY
or
INTELLIGENCE SUMMARY.
(Erase heading not required.)

Army Form C. 2118.

Instructions regarding War Diaries and Intelligence Summaries are contained in F. S. Regs., Part II. and the Staff Manual respectively. Title pages will be prepared in manuscript.

Hour, Date, Place	Summary of Events and Information	Remarks and references to Appendices
DICKEBUSCHE 5-7-15	as on 4-7-15	F M Bury
DICKEBUSCHE 6-7-15	as on 5-7-15	F M Bury
DICKEBUSCHE 7-7-15	Trench Stores & noting a dugout for Enemy station by day. At night improving parapets in front trenches & improving defences on VIERSTRAAT & VORMEZEELE lines & dugong communication trenches	F M Bury
DICKEBUSCHE 8-7-15	as on 7-7-15	F M Bury

WAR DIARY or INTELLIGENCE SUMMARY.

Army Form C. 2118.

Instructions regarding War Diaries and Intelligence Summaries are contained in F. S. Regs., Part II. and the Staff Manual respectively. Title pages will be prepared in manuscript.

(Erase heading not required.)

Hour, Date, Place	Summary of Events and Information	Remarks and references to Appendices
DICKEBUSCHE 9-7-15	as on 8-7-15	H/M maps
DICKEBUSCHE 10-7-15	By day making trench stores. By night working on strong point in P. trench & supervising infantry on supporting lines	H/M maps
DICKEBUSCHE 11-7-15	Attended church parade. At night as on 10-7-15	H/M maps
DICKEBUSCHE 12-7-15	as on 10-7-15	H/M maps
DICKEBUSCHE 13-7-15	as on 12-7-15	H/M maps
DICKEBUSCHE 14-7-15	Packing wagons etc prior to moving billets. NCOs instructed in use of bombs & grenades. Superintending working party on VIERSTRAAT line at night	H/M maps

WAR DIARY or INTELLIGENCE SUMMARY.

Army Form C. 2118.

(Erase heading not required.)

Hour, Date, Place	Summary of Events and Information	Remarks and references to Appendices
KEMMEL 15-7-15	Employed in loading & unloading stores for RE Park. Moved at 8pm to bivouac near KEMMEL	J.M.Meagher
KEMMEL 16-7-15	Loading & unloading stores for RE Park. Officers reconnoitring trenches	J.M.Meagher
LOCRE 17-7-15	Making trench stores. Officers reconnoitring trenches. Moved in afternoon to bivouac in LOCRE	J.M.Meagher
LOCRE 18-7-15	Making trench stores & repairing road in RE Park. Making dug outs for Battle H.Q's at REGENTS DUGOUTS. At night making dug outs for Battle H.Q's G.O.L Sn. J.B. at KEMMEL. Supervising Infantry training trenches	J.M.Meagher
DRANOUTRE 19-7-15	Making trench stores & mining cases. Officers reconnoitring trenches. At night making battle H.Q's G.O.L Sn. J.B. Moved into huts at DRANOUTRE	J.M.Meagher

WAR DIARY
or
INTELLIGENCE SUMMARY.
(Erase heading not required.)

Army Form C. 2118.

Instructions regarding War Diaries and Intelligence Summaries are contained in F. S. Regs., Part II. and the Staff Manual respectively. Title pages will be prepared in manuscript.

Hour, Date, Place	Summary of Events and Information	Remarks and references to Appendices
DRANOUTRE 20-7-15	Making trench stores & mining cases & road in RE Park. Dugouts making dug outs for 2nd 84th I.B. by day & night. Dismantling hut at DICKEBUSCH	J M Mayne
DRANOUTRE 21-7-15	Making trench stores & mining cases & road in RE Park. Erecting hut removed from DICKEBUSCH at BUS FARM. Erecting Battle HdQrs to GOC at KEMMEL. Dug outs for in 85th I.B. trenches. Selecting & superintending cutting of timber for Infantry Battn Dug outs at KEMMEL. Officers reconnoitring & reporting on Supporting Points (10 in number)	J M Mayne

WAR DIARY or INTELLIGENCE SUMMARY.

Army Form C. 2118.

Instructions regarding War Diaries and Intelligence Summaries are contained in F.S. Regs., Part II. and the Staff Manual respectively. Title pages will be prepared in manuscript.

(Erase heading not required.)

Hour, Date, Place	Summary of Events and Information	Remarks and references to Appendices
DRANOUTRE 22-7-15	Day Making trench stores & mining cases Erecting hut at BUS FARM Making battle HdQrs for GOC at KEMMEL Assisting Infantry to dig out dugouts at KEMMEL Night 4 Loopholes fixed in D trenches 2 machine gun loopholes fixed in E, & 15 trenches	H M Magor
DRANOUTRE 23-7-15	Day Making trench stores & mining cases Erecting hut for GOC 85" ID at BUS FARM Making battle HdQrs for GOC at KEMMEL Assisting in dug outs for Infantry Battalion at KEMMEL Night erecting barbed wire entanglement between E, & E6. Supervising Infantry digging dugouts at KEMMEL	H M Magor H M Magor

(9 29 6) W 3332—1107 100,000 10/13 H W V Forms/C. 2118/10.

WAR DIARY
or
INTELLIGENCE SUMMARY.

(Erase heading not required.)

Army Form C. 2118.

Instructions regarding War Diaries and Intelligence Summaries are contained in F. S. Regs., Part II. and the Staff Manual respectively. Title pages will be prepared in manuscript.

Hour, Date, Place	Summary of Events and Information	Remarks and references to Appendices
DRANOUTRE 24-7-15	<u>Day</u> Making trench stores & mining cases Working in dug outs for Infantry Battalion at KEMMEL Making huts for B mess 28th Division <u>Night</u> Dir loopholes fixed into F trenches	F M Napier
DRANOUTRE 25-7-15	<u>Day</u> Making trench stores & mining cases Completed Battle Hd Qrs at KEMMEL Working in dugouts for Infantry Battalion at KEMMEL Making hut for B mess 28th Divn <u>Night</u> 5 loopholes put into G trenches & parapet renewed Supervising Infantry working party on VIERSTRAAT line	F M Napier

WAR DIARY
or
INTELLIGENCE SUMMARY.
(Erase heading not required.)

Army Form C. 2118.

Instructions regarding War Diaries and Intelligence Summaries are contained in F. S. Regs., Part II. and the Staff Manual respectively. Title pages will be prepared in manuscript.

Hour, Date, Place	Summary of Events and Information	Remarks and references to Appendices
DRANOUTRE 26.7.15	Day Truck stores & mining cases Roofing Dugouts for Battn at KEMMEL Making hut for B mess 28th Divn Night Wiring completed between E1 & E6 trenches & small work in right of E1 11 looppholes fixed in this work & E1L Dismantling house in KEMMEL & Supervising Infantry working on VIERSTRAAT line	HWBrown Major
DRANOUTRE 27.7.15	Day Truck stores & mining cases Roofing Dugouts for Infantry at KEMMEL Making hut for B mess 28th Division Night Continuing work on E1 & E2 5 looppholes fixed Supervising Infantry working on VIERSTRAAT line	HWBrown

WAR DIARY
or
INTELLIGENCE SUMMARY.

(Erase heading not required.)

Army Form C. 2118.

Instructions regarding War Diaries and Intelligence Summaries are contained in F. S. Regs., Part II. and the Staff Manual respectively. Title pages will be prepared in manuscript.

Hour, Date, Place	Summary of Events and Information	Remarks and references to Appendices
DRANOUTRE 28-7-15	**Day** Trench stores & mining cases. Roofing Dug outs for Infy at KEMMEL Supervising Infantry on VIERSTRAAT line Mines reconnoitring & trenches **Night** Supervising Infantry working on VIERSTRAAT line	H M Bridger Major
DRANOUTRE 29-7-15	**Day** Trench stores & mining cases. Roofing Dug outs for Infantry at KEMMEL Supervising Infantry on VIERSTRAAT line Blocking up old sap in E, L. **Night** Continuing work in E, & E 2 putting in overhead cover. Supervising Infantry on VIERSTRAAT line & erecting barbed wire in front Putting in 2 machine gun cupolas in H trenches	H M Bridger Major

WAR DIARY or INTELLIGENCE SUMMARY.

Army Form C. 2118.

Hour, Date, Place	Summary of Events and Information	Remarks and references to Appendices
DRANOUTRE 30-7-15	Day — Making trench stores & mining cases. Supervising Infantry working on VIERSTRAAT line. Laying water pipes for supply near Croix de POPERINGHE.	
	Night — Supervising Infantry on VIERSTRAAT line. Continuing work on E trenches.	H M Bragg
DRANOUTRE 31-7-15	Day — Making trench stores & mining cases. Supervising Infantry working on VIERSTRAAT line. Laying water pipes for water supply as above. Continuing huts for Diff Batt 85th IB on KEMMEL HILL. Blocking up sap in E, L.	
	Night — Supervising Infantry on VIERSTRAAT line	H M Bragg

H M Bragg Major
1-8-15 O C 58 (Durham) Coy

28th Division

121/6743

38th Field Coy. R.E.

Vol XIII

August 15

✓

War Diary
38th Field Company RE
from 1st August 1915 to 31st August 1915

Volume 1

WAR DIARY
or
INTELLIGENCE SUMMARY.

(Erase heading not required.)

Instructions regarding War Diaries and Intelligence Summaries are contained in F. S. Regs., Part II. and the Staff Manual respectively. Title pages will be prepared in manuscript.

Army Form C. 2118.

Hour, Date, Place		Summary of Events and Information	Remarks and references to Appendices
DRANOUTRE 1-8-15	By day	Making trench stores & mining cases Blocking up Sap in E.L. Erecting huts for Battalion 85th Inf. Brigade Roofing Dugouts for Battalion 84th Inf. Brigade Supervising Infantry on VIERSTRAAT line	
	By night	Erecting barbed wire & supervising Infantry on VIERSTRAAT line Fixing M.G. Loophole in H4	F M Bnapn
DRANOUTRE 2-8-15	By day	As on 1-8-15	
	By night	Supervising Infantry on VIERSTRAAT line	F M Bnapn
DRANOUTRE 3-8-15	By day	Making trench stores & mining cases Collecting material for water supply CHATEAU DOUVE Erecting huts for QoG 85th I.B. Erecting huts for Battn 85th I.B. Supervising Infantry on VIERSTRAAT line	
	night	Erecting barbed wire on VIERSTRAAT line Adjusting loopholes in E trenches	F M Bnapn

WAR DIARY or INTELLIGENCE SUMMARY.

Army Form C. 2118.

(Erase heading not required.)

Instructions regarding War Diaries and Intelligence Summaries are contained in F. S. Regs., Part II. and the Staff Manual respectively. Title pages will be prepared in manuscript.

Hour, Date, Place		Summary of Events and Information	Remarks and references to Appendices
DRANOUTRE 4-8-15	Day	Making trench stores & mining cases Laying water supply at CHATEAU DOUVE Erecting hut for GOC 85th IB Erecting huts for Battn 85th IB. Making knife rests for VIERSTRAAT line	
	Night	Supervising Infantry on VIERSTRAAT line Improving drainage of C. trenches damaged by mine	J.M.B. Major
DRANOUTRE 5-8-15	Day	Making trench stores & mining cases Laying water supply at CHATEAU DOUVE Erecting hut for GOC 85th IB Erecting huts for Battn 85th IB. Erecting barbed wire on VIERSTRAAT line	
	Night	Supervising Infantry on VIERSTRAAT line Reconnoitring & laying out support trench in rear of C trenches	J.M.B. Major

WAR DIARY or INTELLIGENCE SUMMARY.

Army Form C. 2118.

Instructions regarding War Diaries and Intelligence Summaries are contained in F. S. Regs., Part II. and the Staff Manual respectively. Title pages will be prepared in manuscript.

(*Erase heading not required.*)

Hour, Date, Place		Summary of Events and Information	Remarks and references to Appendices
DRANOUTRE 6-8-14	Day	Making trench stores & mining cases Laying water supply at CHATEAU DOUVE Erecting hut for GOC 85th I.B. Erecting huts for Batt's 85th I.B. Erecting barbed wire & cutting gaps in VIERSTRAAT line Revetting firing steps in VIERSTRAAT line	*signature*
DRANOUTRE 7-8-14	Day	Making trench stores & mining cases Laying water supply at CHATEAU DOUVE Erecting hut for GOC 85th I.B. Erecting huts for Batt's 85th I.B. Erecting barbed wire & cutting gaps in VIERSTRAAT line Cutting gaps in barbed wire in WULVERGHEM sector Supervising Infantry in VIERSTRAAT line	
	Night	Repairing pumps in E trenches Supervising Infantry in VIERSTRAAT line	*signature*

WAR DIARY
or
INTELLIGENCE SUMMARY
(Erase heading not required.)

Army Form C. 2118.

Instructions regarding War Diaries and Intelligence Summaries are contained in F. S. Regs., Part II. and the Staff Manual respectively. Title pages will be prepared in manuscript.

Hour, Date, Place		Summary of Events and Information	Remarks and references to Appendices
DRANOUTRE 8-8-15	Day	Making trench stores & mining cases. Laying water supply at CHATEAU DOUVE. Erecting huts for Battn 85th IB. Erecting hut for G.O.C. 85th IB. Erecting barbed wire & cutting gaps in VIERSTRAAT line. Cutting gaps in wire on WULVERGHEM switch. Filling in sap in E₂ trench & draining communication trench. Supervising Infantry on VIERSTRAAT line.	
	Night	Supervising Infantry on VIERSTRAAT line	F.M.Mayn
DRANOUTRE 9-8-15		As on 8-8-15	F.M.Mayn
DRANOUTRE 10-8-15	Day	Making trench stores & mining cases. Laying water supply at CHATEAU DOUVE. Erecting huts for 85th I.B. Erecting hut for G.O.C. 85th IB. Making hut for G.S. 28th Divn. Draining communication trench behind E₂.	
	Night	Supervising Infantry on VIERSTRAAT line & WULVERGHEM switch.	F.M.Mayn

WAR DIARY
or
INTELLIGENCE SUMMARY.
(Erase heading not required.)

Army Form C. 2118.

Instructions regarding War Diaries and Intelligence Summaries are contained in F. S. Regs., Part II. and the Staff Manual respectively. Title pages will be prepared in manuscript.

Hour, Date, Place		Summary of Events and Information	Remarks and References to Appendices
DRANOUTRE 11-8-15	Day	Making trench stores & mining cases. Completed water supply at CHATEAU DOUVE. Erecting huts for Battn 85th I.B. Erecting hut for G.O.C. 85th I.B. Making hut for G.S. 28th Division. Erecting barbed wire on VIERSTRAAT line. Roofing shell trenches in rear of D trenches. Concreting M.G. emplacement in C₂. Supervising Infantry on VIERSTRAAT line.	
	Night	Concreting M.G. emplacement in C₂. Supervising Infantry on VIERSTRAAT line & WULVERGHEM switch.	J M Bragn
DRANOUTRE 12-8-15	Day	Making trench stores & mining cases. Completed hut for G.O.C. 85th I.B. Erecting huts for Battn 85th I.B. Making hut for G.S. 28th Division. Erecting barbed wire on VIERSTRAAT line. Filling gaps in WULVERGHEM switch. Draining E₂ trenches. Concreting M.G. emplacement in C.	
	Night	As on 11-8-15	J M Bragn

WAR DIARY or INTELLIGENCE SUMMARY

Army Form C. 2118.

Instructions regarding War Diaries and Intelligence Summaries are contained in F. S. Regs., Part II. and the Staff Manual respectively. Title pages will be prepared in manuscript.

(*Erase heading not required.*)

Hour, Date, Place		Summary of Events and Information	Remarks and References to Appendices
DRANOUTRE 13-8-15	Day	Making trench strons & mining cases Erecting huts for Batt⁰ 85th I.B. Erecting hut for G.S. 25th Div⁰ Erecting barbed wire on VIERSTRAAT line Filling gaps in WULVERGHEM switch Supervising Infantry on VIERSTRAAT line	
	night	Cementing M.G. emplacement in C2 Supervising Infantry on VIERSTRAAT line & WULVERGHEM switch Erecting barbed wire on VIERSTRAAT line	HMMayn
DRANOUTRE 14-8-15	Day	as on 13-8-11	
	night	Supervising Infantry on VIERSTRAAT line & WULVERGHEM switch	HMMayn
DRANOUTRE 15-8-15	Day	Making trench stores & mining cases Erecting huts for Batt⁰ 85th I.B. Erecting hut for G.S. 25th Div⁰ Erecting barbed wire on VIERSTRAAT line Supervising Infantry on VIERSTRAAT line	
	night	Supervising Infantry on WULVERGHEM switch Putting in loopholes in E. 14 & 15 trenches	HMMayn

WAR DIARY or INTELLIGENCE SUMMARY.

Army Form C. 2118.

Instructions regarding War Diaries and Intelligence Summaries are contained in F. S. Regs., Part II. and the Staff Manual respectively. Title pages will be prepared in manuscript.

(Erase heading not required.)

Hour, Date, Place		Summary of Events and Information	Remarks and References to Appendices
DRANOUTRE 16-8-15	Day	Making trench stores & mining cases Erecting huts for Batt. 85th I.B. Erecting hut for GS 28th Div Erecting barbed wire on VIERSTRAAT line Filling gaps on WULVERGHEM switch Commenced concreting m.g. emplacement in D4	
	Night	Concreting m.g. emplacement in D4 Supervising Infantry on VIERSTRAAT line	[signature]
DRANOUTRE 17-8-15	Day	Making trench stores & mining cases Erecting huts Supervising Infantry on VIERSTRAAT line & WULVERGHEM switch Concreting m.g. emplacement in D4	
	Night	Concreting m.g. emplacement in D4 Supervising Infantry on VIERSTRAAT line	[signature]

WAR DIARY or INTELLIGENCE SUMMARY.

Army Form C. 2118.

(Erase heading not required.)

Hour, Date, Place	Summary of Events and Information	Remarks and references to Appendices
DRANOUTRE 18-8-15	Day — Making trench stores & mining cases. Erecting huts. Erecting barbed wire on VIERSTRAAT line. Supervising Infantry on VIERSTRAAT line & WULVERGHEM switch. Concreting m.g. emplacement in D4. Night — Supervising Infantry. Concreting m.g. emplacement in D4. Erecting barbed wire on WULVERGHEM switch.	J M Monaghan
DRANOUTRE 19-8-15	Day — Making trench stores & mining cases. Repairing pumps. Erecting huts. Supervising Infantry on WULVERGHEM switch. Supervising Infantry on VIERSTRAAT line. Concreting m.g. emplacement in VIERSTRAAT line. Night — Concreting m.g. emplacement in D4. M.g. emplacement in VIERSTRAAT line. Supervising Infantry on ——.	J M Monaghan

WAR DIARY or INTELLIGENCE SUMMARY.

Army Form C. 2118.

Instructions regarding War Diaries and Intelligence Summaries are contained in F.S. Regs., Part II. and the Staff Manual respectively. Title pages will be prepared in manuscript.

(Erase heading not required.)

Hour, Date, Place		Summary of Events and Information	Remarks and references to Appendices
DRANOUTRE 20-8-15	Day	Making trench stores & mining cases Erecting huts Erecting barbed wire on VIERSTRAAT line Supervising Infantry — Supervising Infantry WOLVERGHEM sector M.G. emplacement on VIERSTRAAT line	
	Night	Supervising Infantry on VIERSTRAAT line	J M Br[...]
DRANOUTRE 21-8-15	Day	Making trench stores & mining cases Erecting huts Erecting barbed wire VIERSTRAAT line Supervising Infantry on VIERSTRAAT line M.G. emplacement on " Repairing pumps	
	Night	Supervising Infantry on VIERSTRAAT line Laying out communication trench	J M Br[...]
DRANOUTRE 22-8-15	Day	As on 21-8-15	
	Night	Do	J M Br[...]

WAR DIARY
or
INTELLIGENCE SUMMARY.

(Erase heading not required.)

Army Form C. 2118.

Instructions regarding War Diaries and Intelligence Summaries are contained in F. S. Regs., Part II. and the Staff Manual respectively. Title pages will be prepared in manuscript.

Hour, Date, Place		Summary of Events and Information	Remarks and References to Appendices
DRANOUTRE 23-8-15	Day	Trench stores & mining cases Erecting huts Supervising Infantry on VIERSTRAAT line Supervising Infantry on WOLVERGHEM switch Making M.G. emplacement on VIERSTRAAT line	
	Night	Making communication trench	J M Magan
DRANOUTRE 24-8-15		as on 23-8-15	J M Magan
DRANOUTRE 25-8-15	~~Day~~	~~as~~ as on 24-8-15	J M Magan
DRANOUTRE 26-8-15	Day	Making trench stores & mining cases Erecting huts Supervising Infantry on VIERSTRAAT line Supervising Infantry on WOLVERGHEM switch Concreting M.G. emplacement on VIERSTRAAT line Supervising Infantry on VIA GELLIA	
	Night	Commenced concrete M.G. emplacement in D.	J M Magan

WAR DIARY ~~or INTELLIGENCE SUMMARY.~~

Army Form C. 2118

Instructions regarding War Diaries and Intelligence Summaries are contained in F. S. Regs., Part II. and the Staff Manual respectively. Title pages will be prepared in manuscript.

(*Erase heading not required.*)

Hour, Date, Place		Summary of Events and Information	Remarks and References to Appendices
DRANOUTRE 27-8-15	Day	Making trench stones & mining cases Erecting huts Supervising Infantry on VIERSTRAAT line Supervising Infantry on WULVERGHEM switch Supervising Infantry on VIA GELLIA Constructing M.G. emplacement in D.	
	night	Supervising Infantry on VIERSTRAAT line Revetting communication trench	HMMaguire
DRANOUTRE 28-8-15		as on 27-8-15	HMMaguire
DRANOUTRE 29-8-15	Day	as on 28-8-15	
	night	Supervising Infantry on VIERSTRAAT line Constructing M.G. emplacement in D.	HMMaguire
DRANOUTRE 30-8-15		as on 29-8-15	HMMaguire

Hour, Date, Place		Summary of Events and Information	Remarks and References to Appendices
DRANOUTRE 31-8-15	Day	Making trench stores & mining cases	
		Erecting huts	
		Supervising Infantry in VIERSTRAAT line	
		Supervising Infantry in WULVERGHEM switch	
		Erecting barbed wire in VIERSTRAAT line	
		Erecting barbed wire in WULVERGHEM switch	
		Laying trench tram lines	
	Night	Supervising Infantry in VIERSTRAAT line	JMM
		Concreting mg emplacement in D,	

2/9/15

J M Burn Major
O C 35 (Welsh) Coy

28th / Division

121/7049

38th Field Coy. RE.

Vol XIV

Sept. 15

✓

WAR DIARY
or
INTELLIGENCE SUMMARY.
(Erase heading not required.)

Army Form C. 2118.

Instructions regarding War Diaries and Intelligence Summaries are contained in F. S. Regs., Part II. and the Staff Manual respectively. Title pages will be prepared in manuscript.

Hour, Date, Place		Summary of Events and Information	Remarks and References to Appendices
DRANOUTRE 1-9-15	Day	Making trench stores & mining cases Erecting barbed wire on VIERSTRAAT line Supervising Infantry on VIERSTRAAT line Erecting barbed wire on WULVERGHEM switch Supervising Infantry on WULVERGHEM switch Laying trench tramways	
	Night	Supervising Infantry on VIERSTRAAT line Completing MG emplacement in D.	Fine, ?may
DRANOUTRE 2-9-15	Day	As on 1-9-15	
	Night	Supervising Infantry on VIERSTRAAT line, little progress owing to bad weather	?m?s
DRANOUTRE 3-9-15	Day	Making trench stores & mining cases Erecting barbed wire on ~~VIERSTRAAT~~ l. WULVERGHEM switch Supervising Infantry on VIERSTRAAT line Supervising Infantry on WULVERGHEM switch Laying trench tramway	Very wet

WAR DIARY or INTELLIGENCE SUMMARY.

Army Form C. 2118.

Instructions regarding War Diaries and Intelligence Summaries are contained in F.S. Regs., Part II. and the Staff Manual respectively. Title pages will be prepared in manuscript.

(Erase heading not required.)

Hour, Date, Place		Summary of Events and Information	Remarks and references to Appendices
DRANOUTRE 4-9-15	Day	Trench Stores & mining cases Erecting barbed wire on WULVERGHEM switch Supervising Infantry on Subsidiary lines Laying trench tramways.	
	night	Erecting barbed wire & supervising Infantry on VIERSTRAAT line	HMBmajor
DRANOUTRE 5-9-15	Day	Making trench stores & mining cases Supervising Infantry on Subsidiary lines. Laying trench tramways C, damaged by mine	
	night	Repairing parapet in C, ~~WOLVERGHEM switch~~ Supervising Infantry on VIERSTRAAT line	HMBmajor
DRANOUTRE 6-9-15	Day	Making trench stores & mining cases Supervising Infantry on Subsidiary lines Drainage work in C trenches Laying trench tramways.	
	night	Laying out support line in E trenches	HMBmajor
DRANOUTRE 7-9-15	Day	Making trench stores & mining cases Supervising Infantry on subsidiary lines Drainage work in C trenches Laying trench tramway cutting in g. emplacement in F 5-	
	night	Reconnoitring & laying out trenches in 84th Brigade area	HMBmajor

WAR DIARY or INTELLIGENCE SUMMARY

Army Form C. 2118.

(Erase heading not required.)

Hour, Date, Place		Summary of Events and Information	Remarks and references to Appendices
DRANOUTRE 8-9-15	Day	Making mining cases & trench struts. Supervising Infantry on WULVERGHEM switch. Laying trench tramways. Drainage work in C trenches Supervising Infantry in VIA GELLIA & KINGSWAY ~~Laying trench tramways~~	
	night	Concreting m.g. emplacement in F5 Rebuilding parapet in G2	FMMmajor
DRANOUTRE 9-9-15	Day	as on 8-9-15	
	night	Superintending Infantry digging communication trenches	FMMmajor
DRANOUTRE 10-9-15	Day	Making trench struts & mining cases Drainage work in C trenches Drainage work in E trenches Concreting m.g. emplacement in F5 Supervising Infantry on subsidiary line Erecting huts on KEMMEL HILL	
	night	Making Artillery Observation Station	FMMmajor

WAR DIARY or INTELLIGENCE SUMMARY.

Army Form C. 2118.

Instructions regarding War Diaries and Intelligence Summaries are contained in F.S. Regs., Part II. and the Staff Manual respectively. Title pages will be prepared in manuscript.

(Erase heading not required.)

Hour, Date, Place		Summary of Events and Information	Remarks and references to Appendices
DRANOUTRE 11-9-15	Day	Making trench stores & mining cases Supervising Infantry on subsidiary line Laying trench tramways Drainage work in C trenches Drainage work in E trenches Concreting M.G. emplacement in F5	
	Night	Concreting M.G. emplacement in F5	HMMmajor
DRANOUTRE 12-9-15	As	on 11-9-15	
DRANOUTRE 13-9-15	Day	Making trench stores & mining cases Laying trench tramways Drainage work in C trenches Supervising Infantry on VIA GELLIA & KINGSWAY Roofing huts on KEMMEL HILL	
	Night	Supervising digging support trenches in rear of E6 Laying trench tramways Concreting M.G. emplacement in F5	HMMmajor

WAR DIARY or INTELLIGENCE SUMMARY

Army Form C. 2118

Instructions regarding War Diaries and Intelligence Summaries are contained in F. S. Regs., Part II. and the Staff Manual respectively. Title Pages will be prepared in manuscript.

(Erase heading not required.)

Place	Date	Hour	Summary of Events and Information	Remarks and references to Appendices
DRANOUTRE	14/9/15	Day	Making trench stores & mining cases Making shell trenches in Subsidiary line Drainage work in C Trenches Drainage work in E Trenches Superintending Infantry in VIA CELLIA & KINGSWAY Laying trench tramways Completing huts on KEMMEL HILL Concreting m.g. emplacement in F5	
		night	Concreting m.g. emplacement in F5 Laying trench tramways	Ymmman Ymmman
DRANOUTRE	15/9/15	Day night	} as on 15-9-15	
DRANOUTRE	16/9/15	Day	Making trench stores & mining cases Drainage work in C Trenches Drainage work in E Trenches Drainage work in WOOD CAMP & erecting huts for Officers there Roofing m.g. emplacement in VIERSTRAAT line Concreting sentry post in D4 trench	
		night	Laying trench tramways Superintending Infantry in KINGSWAY Concreting sentry post in D4	Ymmmayn

WAR DIARY or INTELLIGENCE SUMMARY

Army Form C. 2118

(Erase heading not required.)

Instructions regarding War Diaries and Intelligence Summaries are contained in F. S. Regs., Part II. and the Staff Manual respectively. Title Pages will be prepared in manuscript.

Place	Date	Hour	Summary of Events and Information	Remarks and references to Appendices
DRANOUTRE	17/9/15	Day	Making trench stores & mining cases Drainage work in C Trenches Drainage work in E Trenches Drainage work at WOOD CAMP & erecting huts for Officers these Superintending infantry on VIA GELLIA & KINGSWAY Laying trench tramways erecting huts for Officers at KEMMEL shelters Concreting sentry post in D 4 trench Roofing M.G. emplacement on VIERSTRAAT line	
		night	Laying trench tramways	H.M.may
DRANOUTRE	18/9/15	Day	as on 17-9-15	
		night	Laying trench tramways Concreting sentry post in D 4 erecting barbed wire on WULVERGHEM switch	H.M.may
DRANOUTRE	19/9/15		as on 18-9-15	H.M.may

WAR DIARY or INTELLIGENCE SUMMARY

Army Form C. 2118

Instructions regarding War Diaries and Intelligence Summaries are contained in F. S. Regs., Part II. and the Staff Manual respectively. Title Pages will be prepared in manuscript.

(Erase heading not required.)

Place	Date	Hour	Summary of Events and Information	Remarks and references to Appendices
DRANOUTRE	20/9/15	Day	Making trench stairs Drainage work in C Trenches Drainage work in E Trenches Drainage work in WOOD CAMP Completed mg emplacement in VIERSTRAAT line Superintending Infantry in VIA GELLIA & KINGSWAY. Laying trench tramways Completed concrete sentry post in D4 Officers handing over work to Officers of Canadian Engineers	J M Bragg
		night	no work	
DRANOUTRE	21/9/15	Day	Completed handing over work in chief to Canadian Engineers	J M Bragg
MERRIS	22/9/15		Marched at 10 am to billets in MERRIS Distance 9 miles	J M Bragg
MERRIS	23/9/15		Company employed in overhauling company equipment stores etc	J M Bragg
MERRIS	24/9/15	morning	Company exercise in route marching Distance 8 miles afternoon loading wagons etc	J M Bragg

WAR DIARY or INTELLIGENCE SUMMARY

Army Form C. 2118

Place	Date	Hour	Summary of Events and Information	Remarks and references to Appendices
MERRN	25/9/15	morning	Company exercised in route-marching – distance 11 miles.	W. E. Pile
		afternoon	Loading wagons, company stood by ready to march.	
MERRIS	26/9/15	morning	Marched via STRAZEELE – VIEUX BERQUIN – NEUF BERQUIN – MERVILLE where halted.	W. E. Pile
		afternoon	Continued march via PARADIS – LOCON to BÉTHUNE where billeted. Distance 18 miles	
BETHUNE	27/9/15		Company (less 1 Sec) marched via BEUVRY to SAILLY-LABOURSE where bivouacked in open off road 3/4 mile S.W. of latter. 1 Section marched with 85th I.B. as above thence via NOYELLES to VERMELLES where Infantry ordered to attack. Section stood by, & finally ordered to rejoin company.	W. E. Pile
SAILLY-LABOURSE	28/9/15	morning	Company employed on fatigues.	W. E. Pile
		afternoon	Company proceeded to Railway Reserve Trench for work at night. Two Officers reconnoitred HOHENZOLLERN REDOUBT, but no work could be done. 1 Pioneer wounded.	
SAILLY-LABOURSE	29/9/15		At night dug T-head fire trenches in WEST FACE & SAP L; also wired latter. One Officer & 1 N.C.O. wounded, 3 sappers killed, 1 wounded.	W. E. Pile
SAILLY-LABOURSE	30/9/15		At night continued work in WEST FACE & SAP L, also wired BIG WILLIE. Owing to heavy rifle fire latter could not be completed. 1 N.C.O. injured, 1 N.C.O wounded.	W. E. Pile

28th Division

38th F. Co. R.E.

Oct-15

Vol XV

121/7449

WAR DIARY or INTELLIGENCE SUMMARY

Army Form C. 2118

38th (Field) Coy. R.E.

Instructions regarding War Diaries and Intelligence Summaries are contained in F. S. Regs., Part II. and the Staff Manual respectively. Title Pages will be prepared in manuscript.

(Erase heading not required.)

Place	Date	Hour	Summary of Events and Information	Remarks and references to Appendices
SAILLY-LABOURSE / VERMELLES	1/10/15		Moved from SAILLY-LABOURSE to VERMELLES, leaving transport at SAILLY-LABOURSE. Infantry working party for night work did not arrive. 1 officer and small party marked points for guidance in digging trenches projected.	
VERMELLES	2/10/15		Day-work. Preparing wire entanglements in Quarry opposite HOHENZOLLERN redoubt. Night-work. No work could be done as parties were prevented from getting to site of work by (i) being shelled, which necessitated taking to communication trenches (ii) being blocked in these trenches owing to projected attack (which was constantly postponed) (iii) by attack itself. Parties were thus delayed until it was too late for any work to be done by the time the site could be reached. 1 Section was held in readiness to assist in attack on LITTLE WILLIE by 84th Infantry Brigade, but it was not required.	
VERMELLES	3/10/15		Day-work. As on 2-10-15. Night-work. Superintending infantry working parties digging communication and support trenches behind Big WILLIE. 1 Section held in readiness to assist in attack on WEST FACE of HOHENZOLLERN redoubt, to be made by 83rd Infantry Brigade in event of a section from 101st (Field) Coy. not being at hand in time. This latter section, however, arrived in time; so 38th Coy. section was not required.	
VERMELLES	4/10/15		Resting. 1 officer acted as guide to Pioneer Battalion at night.	
VERMELLES	5/10/15		Night-work. Whole company wiring old British front line from AUCHY road to about 200 ft South of Sap K.	

WAR DIARY or INTELLIGENCE SUMMARY

Army Form C. 2118

Place	Date	Hour	Summary of Events and Information	Remarks and references to Appendices
VERMELLES / L'ECLÈME	6/10/15		Moved to rest area at L'ECLÈME.	
L'ECLÈME	7/10/15		Resting.	
L'ECLÈME	8/10/15		Inspection by G.O.C. I Corps. Captain G. MASTER took over command of company from Lieut. W.E. EULER, who had acting O.C. since Major F.M. BROWNE was wounded on the night of 29/30-9-15. [Major BROWNE died of wounds in hospital on 1-10-15]	
L'ECLÈME	9/10/15		Route march.	
L'ECLÈME	10/10/15		Church parade.	
L'ECLÈME	11/10/15 to 16/10/15		Company employed at pontooning & trestle bridging over canal (by half coys at a time), drill, musketry, semaphore, etc. Search-lights overhauled and tested.	
L'ECLÈME / BETHUNE	17/10/15		Moved to BETHUNE.	
BETHUNE	18/10/15		Reconnoitred trenches for work. Night-work. 2 sections employed wiring and altering communication trench just South of LA BASSÉE road and East of BRADELL'S POINT, [working under C.E. I Corps.]	

WAR DIARY or INTELLIGENCE SUMMARY

Army Form C. 2118

Instructions regarding War Diaries and Intelligence Summaries are contained in F. S. Regs., Part II. and the Staff Manual respectively. Title Pages will be prepared in manuscript.

(Erase heading not required.)

Place	Date	Hour	Summary of Events and Information	Remarks and references to Appendices
BETHUNE / ESSARS	19/10/15		Moved to war ESSARS. Engap work. 2 sections employed, in same vicinity as on 18-10-15, on improving & altering communication trenches, making M.G. emplacement and T-heads.	
ESSARS	20/10/15		Day-work. 2 sections employed, in same vicinity as on 19-10-15, on revetting firing steps, rebuilding traverses, blocking old communication trench, and finishing M.G. emplacement and T-heads, and making gap in brick breast-work. Handed over above work and work projected for future to Officer of E. Anglian Field Coy. R.E. (2nd Division)	
ESSARS	21/10/15		Resting.	
ESSARS	22/10/15		Resting.	
ESSARS / LILLERS / EN ROUTE	23/10/15		Marched to Lillers and entrained there, leaving at 9.51 a.m.	
EN ROUTE / MARSEILLES	24/10/15 25/10/15		Train journey; arrived at Marseilles at about 8.0 pm. Detrained, and marched to camp on racecourse.	
MARSEILLES	26/10/15		Resting.	
MARSEILLES	27/10/15		Resting.	
MARSEILLES	28/10/15		Resting.	
MARSEILLES	29/10/15		Resting.	

WAR DIARY
~~INTELLIGENCE SUMMARY~~

Army Form C. 2118

Instructions regarding War Diaries and Intelligence Summaries are contained in F. S. Regs., Part II. and the Staff Manual respectively. Title Pages will be prepared in manuscript.

Place	Date	~~Hour~~	Summary of Events and Information	Remarks and references to Appendices
MARSEILLES	30/10/15		Resting.	
MARSEILLES	31/10/15		Resting.	
	2-11-15		Forgemaster. Capt. R. Cmdg. 38th (Field) Coy. R.E.	

www.ingramcontent.com/pod-product-compliance
Lightning Source LLC
Chambersburg PA
CBHW081239170426
4319ICB00034B/1976